THE
MILLENNIUM

ENTERTAINMENT

A Pictorial History of the
Past One Thousand Years

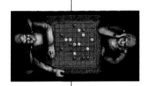

Sue Hamilton

AB&DO
Dau&ters

Visit us at
www.abdopub.com

Published by ABDO Publishing Company, 4940 Viking Drive, Edina, MN 55435.
Copyright ©2000 by Abdo Consulting Group, Inc. International copyrights reserved in all
countries. No part of this book may be reproduced in any form without written permission from
the publisher.

Printed in the United States.

Art Direction: John Hamilton

Cover photos: AP/Wideworld Photos, Corbis
Interior photos: AP/Wideworld Photos, Corbis

Library of Congress Cataloging–in–Publication Data

Hamilton, Sue L., 1959-
     Entertainment / Sue Hamilton.
          p. cm. -- (The millennium)
     Includes index.
     Summary: A pictorial history of developments in entertainment over the last millennium.
     ISBN 1-57765-360-2
     1. Performing arts--Pictorial works--Juvenile literature. 2. Amusements--Pictorial
works--Juvenile literature. [1. Performing arts--History. 2. Amusements--History.] I.
Title. II. Millennium (Minneapolis, Minn.)

PN1584 .H36 2000
791--dc21

                                                99-046928

CONTENTS

INTRODUCTION

The great Greek philosopher Plato said, "Life must be lived as play." Amasis I, King of Egypt, said, "If they [Egyptians] give themselves continuously to serious work . . . they lose their senses and become mad, or moody." A Roman writer, Decimus Junius Juvenalis, said that people wanted "panem et circenses"—bread and circuses. As long as humans have lived, they have sought to have fun. In some ways, sources of entertainment have changed little through the ages.

Music, song, and dance have existed for as long as can be remembered, yet continue to entertain people as a new millennium dawns.

Challenges in sports have proven who is the greatest athlete from ancient days to modern Olympics.

Actors have made audiences laugh and cry in theaters, ranging from open air stadiums to modern motion picture theaters.

Exaggerated stunts and costumed performances by acrobats, jugglers, and clowns entertained early civilizations and continue to do so.

There is no question that some forms of entertainment are very different but as we look at the pleasures and pastimes of people of the past, take note of how fun has changed and yet has stayed the same.

BEFORE THE MILLENNIUM

Even though early humans spent much of their time just trying to survive, they still sought ways to enjoy themselves.

Earliest people sang songs and created music using whatever materials they could find. Dancing has appeared in prehistoric cave art.

Some games and sports created in ancient times have survived to modern times. Ancient peoples around the world gambled with dice of different materials and shapes. In 776 B.C., the ancient Greeks created the Olympian Games as part of a national festival. These games are the inspiration for today's Olympics.

Few hand written books were available, but stories were told over and over, combining entertainment with history and education. People used their imaginations, abilities, and raw materials at hand to create their entertainment.

The Stone Age

Earliest people used such things as tree branches, conch shells, and animal horns and bones to make music.

Whether for fun or as a religious ritual, prehistoric cave paintings from the Paleolithic or Stone Age (20,000-plus years ago) show figures dancing in animal costumes.

Bone Flutes

The Egyptians

Magic was performed for Egyptian pharaohs some 4,500 years ago. Magician Weba-aner turned a small wax model of a crocodile into a live, fully grown, ferocious animal.

Senet was an Egyptian race game and may be the ancestor of modern backgammon. The popularity of this game is evident from the number of sets that have been found in Egyptian tombs.

The oldest known representation of Senet is in a painting from the tomb of Hesy (2650 B.C.).

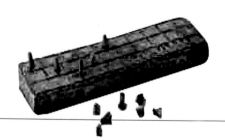

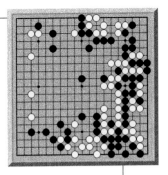

The Chinese

China's game of GO may be the world's oldest board game, with references going back to 2356 B.C. It spread to Japan and became their most popular game. The objective is to surround an opponent's pieces. Some ancient rules include: Sit up straight—do not lean over the board. Do not blow smoke in your opponent's face. In victory, do not gloat.

When an Indian priest and knight, Bodhidharma, brought Zen Buddhism to China in the early sixth century, he also introduced a system of 18 self-defense exercises. These movements grew into the martial arts, which were used both as a sport and a type of unarmed combat.

The Greeks

During the Olympian Games, ancient Greeks participated in the pentathlon. This consisted of five events: sprinting, long jumping, javelin hurling, discus throwing, and wrestling. Winners were given a crown of wild olive branches, had poems written about them, and were often taken care of for the rest of their lives.

Bull leapers, around 1600 B.C., on the Greek island of Crete were young Minoan men and women who would grab the horns of charging bulls and vault over the animals' heads. They became popular and wealthy stars, often wearing colorful costumes that became a central part of entertainment as we know it.

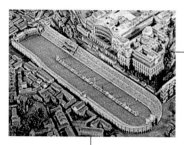

The Romans

From 600 B.C. to the sixth century A.D., Romans came to huge stadiums to watch chariot races or to see gladiators take on wild animals and even each other. Julius Caesar created an arena in ancient Rome known as Circus Maximus. This held 200,000 spectators — today's stadiums usually hold about 75,000 people.

Tali, commonly known today as Knucklebones, was a popular board game. It resembled the game of dice except that sets of marked bones, called tali, were used. Tali was inherited from the Ancient Greeks, who originally made the pieces from astragali, or the knucklebones of sheep or goats. The Romans also made them from silver, gold, ivory, marble, wood, bone, bronze, glass, terra-cotta, and precious gems. The original shape of the tali, however, was preserved. These shapes would sit on one of four sides when dropped.

On the vase above, women are playing tali.

Duodecim Scripta means "Twelve Lines" and was played on a board like the one below. Two players sat across from each other and placed their 15 black or white pieces on the first square on their side of the board. They then each tossed a set of three dice from a cup and would move their pieces according to the value of the throw. The object was to get all of one's pieces across the board to the final square.

Playing dice was another popular game. Dice were shaken in a cup and then tossed. Bets were placed in the same manner as we place them today.

I	II	III	IV	V	VI	VII	VIII	IX	X	XI	XII
XXIV	XXIII	XXII	XXI	XX	XIX	XIIX	XVII	XVI	XV	XIV	XIII

In this tile mosaic (right), two Romans from North Africa play dice on a table suspended across their knees. The pair of dice shown at right was found at Herculaneum.

8

India

Chess is believed to have come from chaturanga, a game that originated in India in the sixth century. The game board represents a battlefield, and chaturanga refers to the four divisions of an Indian army—elephants, cavalry, chariots, and infantry—thus the four different playing pieces. The game quickly spread to the surrounding countries, and was very well known in Europe by the end of the tenth century.

The Aztecs

Ancient Aztecs played a game like basketball with a rubber ball. In Chichén Itzá, there is a court 540 feet (168 m) by 224 feet (68 m), dating back at least a thousand years.

The Aztecs threw a rubber ball through this ring.

The Vikings

Hnefatafl is an ancient Viking siege game which dates back to the fifth century. The Vikings brought it to their colonies in Ireland, Iceland, Greenland, England, and Wales.

The objective of the white pieces is to try to get your king to escape to the corner or edge squares of the board. The objective of the black pieces is to capture the white king. The pieces move like rooks in chess. Captures are usually accomplished by surrounding one of your opponents pieces on two sides with two of your own pieces.

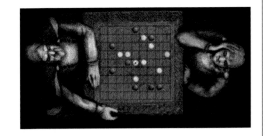

THE 1000s

The turn of the century was a time of learning and growth, but also a time of war. Most entertainment during this time centered around skills necessary to survive—strength, quickness, and cunning. People used what creativity and resources they had available to create games and challenges. Books were still mostly in the hands of the church and the wealthy, so common people remembered their history and their adventures through stories and songs that were told over and over.

Storytelling

Professional storytellers, or scops, traveled to villages telling tales in return for food and money. Another word for a poet or storyteller was "hearpere" (harper). This person probably used a harp to add emphasis to his story, or as background music. Not only the scops told stories, but everybody did. The ability to tell a story was highly valued. Most stories were of famous people or great heroes. Vikings told great stories called sagas.

Riddles

Along with storytelling, a popular pastime was riddling. A warrior was judged by not only how good he was with weapons, but also how good he was with words. Riddles described everyday objects in an unusual way, and could be from one to 100 lines long. Here are some actual Saxon riddles:

"I'm told a certain object grows in the corner, rises and expands, throws up a crust.

A proud wife carried off that boneless wonder, the daughter of a king covered that swollen thing with a cloth."

Answer: Dough/bread

Music

Gleemen, or professional musicians, traveled around singing for money. Musical ability was considered a good kingly skill, and many royals were buried with musical instruments. It was common for everyone to take part in the singing and music-making. After a feast, a harp would be passed around the hall so that each person could take a turn at entertaining. It was very embarrassing to have no music-making skill.

Few actual musical instruments from the eleventh century have survived, although many illustrations show harps, lyres, bone whistles, horns, panpipes, psalteries, and some form of drum. Archaeological digs have found a large number of bone whistles (also called pipe or sangpipe), showing them to have been popular instruments of common people.

Games

People of the eleventh century played many different board games. The word tafl (literally 'table') was used to describe a board game. The pieces were called toflur or hunn. They were made of antler, amber, bone, glass, clay, stone, or even horses' teeth. Rules for many of these games are unknown, and likely would have been different from place to place.

Hnefatafl was probably the most common board game played, and was similar to chess.

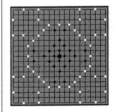

Tafl is one variation of Hnefatafl, an ancient Viking siege game which dates back to the fifth century.

Merels, or Nine Men's Morris, has been known as "the game on the other side of the board." Several boards have had Hnefatafl on one side and Nine Men's Morris on the other. However, the game has also been found in rather unexpected places—ship's timbers, loose boards, benches, lumps of rock and, later, even on church pews and tiles. The name merels comes from the low Latin word *merrelus*, meaning a "token, counter or coin." It was similar to Noughts and Crosses played today.

THE 1100s

Religious wars known as the Crusades continued during the twelfth century, influencing songwriters, poets, and playwrights to compose poems and plays on Christianity and love. Musical instruments were being created and refined. Oppositely, many activities that we today would find quite cruel kept people entertained. Most involved the death or wounding of an animal. Royals and nobility brought back the sport of horse racing which was once popular with ancient Romans.

The contest of troubadours at the Court of Hermann I of Thuringia, Germany

Music

During the twelfth century, French troubadours and German minnesingers became popular. Most troubadours and minnesingers were high-class nobles or kings. They composed and performed a special kind of poetry that celebrated love, heroism, and nature.

Troubadours sang their own poems to their assembled courts or competed against one another in tournaments of song. Later on, low-class but skilled musicians or jongleurs were hired to come and perform the works of accomplished troubadours.

In Germany, the minnesingers sang for the love of it. One famous minnesinger was Walther von der Vogelweide, whose best-known song is "Crusader's Song."

Musical instruments continued to develop. The viele, ancestor of the modern violin, had five strings (unlike today's four-stringed violin) and was used to accompany singers.

The organistrum (right) was a stringed instrument that was played by turning a wheel so the strings would be

muted by a set of bars rather than fingers. It usually required two people to operate, and was most useful in a large church setting.

Feasts & Festivals

People celebrated many feasts and festivals. The Feast of Fools was popular in Europe beginning in the twelfth century. It was held at the beginning of the year. For one day, slaves and masters exchanged roles. It was first celebrated in churches, where subdeacons gained the rank and privileges of the higher clergy.

Sport

In England, public arenas called bear gardens hosted the sport of bearbaiting. A bear was chained to a stake and a pack of dogs was let loose upon it. The bear was almost always killed. Parliament outlawed this activity in 1835.

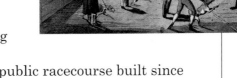

In 1110, King Henry I of England bought an Arabian stallion from Spain. Known for their swiftness, these horses became popular racing animals. In 1174, London's Smithfield Track became the first public racecourse built since the time of Romans. Horse racing is still often referred to as "the sport of kings."

During bird hunts, stones were shot at pigeons and other birds. Many windows and people became the unintended targets of less-than-accurate throwers.

THE 1200s

Fairs with dancing and singing distracted common people from the hardships of their daily lives in the thirteenth century. Sometimes people sang to pass time while performing their work. Their simple songs grew into more complex musical compositions. Religion was important to the people of the thirteenth century—many plays surrounded stories from the Bible. People still engaged in contests of skills and strength, yet they loved to watch the tricks of entertainers.

Fairs

The Fair of St. Denis was held during the month of October in Paris. Merchants came from all over to bring their wares to sell, but they also came to have fun. People watched a conjurer swallow fire or a sword, and laughed at tumblers and jugglers. They also attended dances and sang.

Dance

Carol-dancing was performed in a circle. With hands clasped or arms linked, the dancers circled a leader, who stood in the middle. The leader sang while the dancers moved around. Then, the dancers stood in place and sang a chorus. Caroling was sometimes done outdoors in the churchyard. Clergymen preferred their people to devote themselves to more religious pursuits, and gave out penances for sins of voice, movement, and touching.

Music

Polyphonic music—music with several sounds sung at the same time—spread from the church to the songs of the people in the late twelfth century. The first secular motets were created in France in the thirteenth century.

Plays

Mystery or miracle plays were performances of scenes or stories from the Bible. In 1210, the Roman Catholic church forbade priests from appearing on stage. Thus church dramas about miracles, saints, and other Old and New Testament stories began to be performed by actors.

Sport

Ring-spearing tournaments, or "Tilting at the Quintain," were popular. A horseman would gallop up with his lance pointed toward a ring which hung on brightly colored ribbons from a tree or between two posts. When lanced, the ring slid down the shaft and a stream of ribbons fluttered in the wind. A steady lance, great horsemanship, and a keen eye were all vital to success.

Games

Blind man's bluff, or hoodman blind, was played by children and adults. Whoever was "it" had their eyes covered by turning their hood around.

THE 1300s

The 100 Years' War between England and France began in 1337. From 1347-1350, The Black Death (named because of the dark patches on the skin) killed a third of the population of Europe. Still, beautiful music was played, games were developed and more and more literature was written.

Geoffrey Chaucer

Storytelling

Geoffrey Chaucer (1343-1400), one of the greatest of English poets, produced a famous story known as the *Canterbury Tales*. This was a story about a group of pilgrims making a journey to Canterbury Cathedral. Within the story, each of the pilgrims, in order to pass the time as they traveled, were to make up four tales of their own. Because of this masterpiece of literature, Chaucer is often considered the father of English poetry.

Music

The pear-shaped lute was made with four to ten sheep-gut strings. It was very lightweight and portable.

The Italian cembalo, or harpsichord, was a predecessor to the piano.

Games

Tarot cards were invented in 1320. Originally, they were used to play games. Later, they were used to tell a person's future.

Magic

In 1355, a traveler viewed the Indian Rope Trick, where a rope is thrown into the air, stays there, and a child climbs up.

Sport

Falconry was a sport where birds were taught to catch prey. They hunted small animals such as hares on the ground. They also hunted other birds such as doves in the air. The birds brought their prey back to their master.

Falconry was often a sport of kings and nobles. Some spent huge sums of money on decorated hoods or on bejeweled jesses. The trained birds were quite valuable, and it was required by law that if one was found, it must be turned over to the sheriff to be returned to its owner.

Poaching, or illegally hunting, deer was a way for lower class people to not only gain food and clothing, but also to enjoy the

sport of gentlemen. A game law was enacted in 1390 to protect private forests and parks from peasants. This made hunting even more appealing to a poacher, as he wanted to show that he could get away with it, proving that the owner was weak and that a mere peasant could outwit a nobleman.

Games of skill between knights were known as tournaments. Jousts, or single combats between two knights, were aided with the development of the lance-rest in the second half of the fourteenth century. Attached to the armor's breast plate and looking like a prong, the device helped steady and support the lance. This meant that knights could now use longer and heavier lances, which in turn meant that these tournaments were even more dangerous and exciting than ever!

Plays

Noh drama was created in Japan in the fourteenth century. Kanmi Kiyotsugu and his son Zeami Motokiyo further perfected the artform in 1374, performing for shoguns. Noh dramas are long plays, sometimes lasting for several hours. Male performers used dance, song, mime, and masks to present deeply emotional stories on stage.

THE 1400s

The term Renaissance is applied to this period of history in Western Europe. Art, once flat and one-dimensional, was suddenly very realistic-looking with the work of Leonardo Da Vinci and Michelangelo. The world expanded with Christopher Columbus's trip to America in 1492. The printing of books, beginning with the Gutenberg Bible, suddenly changed how people learned. This was a century of discovery.

Dance

Ballet began in the courts of Italy and France. A dance during a banquet in 1479 was coordinated with the meal. For example, the dance showing the adventure story of Jason and the Golden Fleece preceded the serving of roast lamb.

Music

The clavichord, the oldest form of stringed keyboard instrument, was a predecessor of the piano. The clavichord (left) was popular from the 1400s to the early 1800s and underwent a revival in the twentieth century. It has a rectangular case with the keyboard to the left and the soundboard at the right end.

Minstrels, or professional musicians, were thought to be extremely important members of society. Some were poor, traveling throughout the country, while others lived in luxury, paid to perform by nobles and kings. In 1415, King Henry V went to war in France. He brought his minstrels with him. Each was paid the same as a master surgeon and twice as much as an archer.

Games

European playing cards were first printed in the fifteenth century. France introduced the traditional card suits of heart, club, spade, and diamond.

Billiards was popular in the French court at Versailles. King Louis XI is thought to have been the first to play indoors, purchasing a table in 1470. This led to the game of pool.

Sport

Archery contests were held to determine the greatest marksman. The story of Robin Hood, the heroic outlaw who stole from the rich to give to the poor, originated in the late fourteenth or early fifteenth century. His bow and arrow feats included an ability to split one arrow with another.   It is unknown if he was real or fictional.

Scotland is considered the home of the modern game of golf, first played in the fourteenth or fifteenth century. Instead of practicing military skills such as archery, the Scots preferred their golf. In 1457, Scottish parliament passed a law prohibiting the game.

However, the law was mostly ignored. When Mary (later Mary, queen of Scots) played the game while at school in France, the young men who accompanied her on the course were known as cadets.   The term was later adopted as caddy or caddie — the person who carries the bag of golf clubs around the course.

The sport of angling was printed in the 1496 *Boke of St. Albans* in a chapter called "The Treatyse of fysshynge wyth an Angle." The conclusion was that fishing helped people lead long and satisfying lives, and gave instructions on how to be a better angler.

In the fifteenth century, Russians developed ice slides, the predecessor to roller coasters.   Known as "Russian Mountains," people climbed up wooden stairs to the top, then boarded a sled to blast down the hill. The speed and danger made them popular and the ice-slide phenomenon caught on in surrounding countries.

Books

German printer Johannes Gutenberg is credited with printing the first book in movable type, the Gutenberg Bible (right), in about 1455. This made publishing much quicker and cheaper. Suddenly, people began learning to read.

THE 1500s

Although the world was being opened up by such explorers as Ferdinand Magellan, Juan Ponce de Leon, Francisco Pizarro, and Hernán Cortés, people still spent most of their lives in one place. It has been estimated that the average person saw no more than 100 people in his or her entire lifetime. Imagine the excitement when traveling performers rolled into a village bringing music, theater, laughter, and exotic performances. But entertainers had to be careful—anyone believed to have supernatural abilities could be tried and executed as a witch.

Traveling Performers

Traveling performers turned their wagons into stages, bringing theater to remote villages. In addition, jesters, jugglers, fire-eaters, waterspouters, stoneswallowers, acrobats, contortionists, and men with dancing bears traveled from town to town to perform for rich and poor alike.

Court Jesters

Although fools, also known as jesters, jokers, and buffoons, have entertained for thousands of years, King Henry VIII of England employed a special fool by the name of Will Sommers (right). Will was a very witty man who could recite hundreds of poems, stories, and proverbs. In his position, he enjoyed insulting the top officials of the day. King Henry once said, "William, your tongue is privileged." Fools got away with saying things that others never could. But what made Will Sommers extra special was that he used his position to speak to the king to help the poor.

Music

The violin achieved its present form in about 1550. It was Stradivarius (1644-1737), however, who created what has been called the finest design ever made.

In the late sixteenth century, a group of musicians and scholars who called themselves the *Camerata* created a form of entertainment where a dramatic performance is set to music. Their objective was to revive the style of ancient Greek drama intermixed with a more modern style of music. The music was to reflect the meaning of the story. This became known as opera. In 1597, Jacopo Peri wrote the first opera: *Dafne*. Italian Claudio Monteverdi was the first major composer to apply his talents to this dramatic style.

Executions

One grisly form of entertainment was to watch public executions. As people could be hanged for a great many crimes, including theft or vandalism, there was a never-ending supply of criminals for any day's entertainment. It was believed that showing people what would happen to them if they committed crimes would keep them from performing the same evil deeds.

Plays

William Shakespeare wrote his first play in 1589 at the age of 25. Prior to theaters, plays were performed in the courtyards of inns and taverns. But within 10 years, Shakespeare became a part owner in the new Globe Theater in London. Shakespeare has become known as one of the greatest dramatists of all time. His works continue to be performed today.

A reconstruction of the Globe Theater stage

Games

Boys played with taws or marbles.

Sport

Tennis originated in France in the Middle Ages and was known as the game Jeu de Paume. It became very popular among European noblemen. Henry VIII (1491-1547) of England built a court at his Hampton Court palace, which is still used today.

The rapier was introduced in Italy and quickly became a popular court weapon in the 1500s. Gentlemen settled matters of honor with this sword. From this, the sport of fencing grew. Modern swords include the foil, the epee, and the saber.

The Basques of northern Spain created a type of handball game called *pelota,* Spanish for ball. It later became known as jai alai. First played outdoors using the church walls as the court, the game was later played on a long, narrow, three-walled court. An extremely hard rubber ball is caught and thrown with a cesta, a long, curved wicker scoop strapped to one arm. Deemed the world's fastest ball game, it is also one of the most dangerous. The ball, which is slightly smaller than a baseball and feels like a rock, can be flung at speeds over 180 miles per hour (290 km/h). Many players have been injured and even killed playing jai alai. In 1968, helmets became required equipment.

THE 1600s

The seventeenth century offered many forms of theater in many parts of the world. And the world was opening up with the first American colonists settling in Jamestown, Virginia, in 1607. Life was never easy, but people saw extraordinary dramatic performances, discovered new games, and continued to learn and grow.

Puppets

Japanese bunraku or jorui puppet theater (left) featured half life-size puppets, which were manipulated by onstage puppeteers dressed in black. In addition to the puppets, there were chanters who sang and spoke for the puppets, as well as musicians who accompanied the performers on shamisens. Although growing to great popularity well into the 1700s, bunraku performances eventually lost in public favor to the dramas of Kabuki.

Theater

In 1603, Kabuki theater began in Japan. Ka means "song," bu means "dance," and ki means "skill." Kabuki uses elaborate costumes and stage settings to present vibrant performances. While Noh drama was performed for nobility, Kabuki became theater for the townspeople.

Using mime and brilliant makeup that made the actors appear to wear masks, a type of dance-drama known as kathakali (below, left) developed in India. It was originally presented to the raja, or prince, of Kottarakara. Stories of heroes, villains, gods, and demons are acted out by dancers wearing huge headdresses and costumes. Aside from small grunts, no words are spoken. A series of 24 specific hand gestures or mudras which, when combined, have over 800 meanings, are used to assist in conveying the story.

In seventeenth-century England, dramas featuring mythical characters were presented with actors wearing masks. These plays combined poetry, music and dance and were known as masque. In these performances the audience participated in the dance. However, when Oliver Cromwell became Lord Protector of England in 1653, the theaters were closed as he, a Puritan, thought them to be not very respectable. The theaters reopened in 1660.

A Kabuki performer (above)

Sport

Bowling balls and pins have been found dating back to 5200 B.C. Germans are often credited with creating the modern form, in which they rolled stones at nine wooden clubs called kegles. But it was the Dutch who brought it to America in the 1600s. People began to gamble on the games, and it became known as evil. The state of Connecticut outlawed "bowling at nine pins." To get around the law, players added an additional pin and began the 10-pin game that continues to be played today.

Bowling is played today with ten pins.

Field hockey came from the British games of hurling, bandy, and shinty. The name is thought to come from the French word *hoquet*, meaning a hooked stick.

Lacrosse, a type of field hockey, was first played by North American Indians as part of their training for war. They called it buggataway. French settlers in North America thought the hooked sticks reminded them of a bishop's staff or crozier—thus the name lacrosse.

Dakota Indians used lacrosse to train for war and settle disputes.

Parks & Gardens

Vauxhall Gardens (right) on the River Thames opened in 1661. It became a popular resort for Londoners. The manor was originally owned by Falkes de Breaute, which became Falkes Hall, which slurred into Vauxhall.

Covent Garden was London's first formal square surrounded by townhouses. It was designed in 1632 by English architect Inigo Jones. He originally laid it out as a market where fruit, vegetables, and flowers could be sold.

"Pleasure parks" (left) were popular with people in Europe in the seventeenth century, offering such entertainment as bowling, archery, shuffleboard, singing, dancing, and trained animal acts, plus refreshments.

Music

The acoustic, or Spanish guitar, (right) presented a popularity challenge to the lute in seventeenth-century Europe.

Games

The French played a game of "bridge." Marbles were rolled through little gates to score points.

THE 1700S

Deemed the Age of Enlightenment, the eighteenth century was a time of growth and change in government, as well as in science and the arts. Renowned composers created beautiful music with wondrous instruments. Fabulous dances were developed. Zoos and museums were made available to the public. People learned new games from all around the world.

Circus

In 1768, Philip Astley invented the circus ring in England. A horseman could ride standing up and keep his balance by using the laws of physics — centrifugal force. Astley added trick riders, tumbling, juggling, trained animal performances, and clowns to his program. In 1782, one of Astley's riders, Charles Hughes, coined the word *circus*, which is the Latin word for *ring*. In 1793, John Bill Ricketts, a pupil of Charles Hughes, presented his own circus show in Philadelphia, the largest city in the United States at the time. His performance was attended by President George Washington.

Philip Astley's circus ring

Charles Hughes, a former rider for Philip Astley, opens his own circus.

Music

To overcome a harpsichord's single volume level, in 1709 Bartolomeo Cristofori invented the pianoforte. Depending on how hard or soft a key was pressed, the player could control the sound, which vastly improved the instrument's musical expression. From 1775 to present, pianos have been popular in homes.

Piano Forte

Great composers such as Johann Sebastian Bach (1685-1750), Wolfgang Amadeus Mozart (1756-1791), and Ludwig van Beethoven (1770-1827) performed their masterpieces as concertmasters for churches and court orchestras.

Wolfgang Amadeus Mozart as a young man

The first barrel organ (right) was used in England in the early eighteenth century. It became popular in churches to accompany singers.

German flute maker Johann Denner modified a reedpipe to invent the clarinet in 1700. By 1780, clarinets were common in orchestras.

Benjamin Franklin created the glass harmonica in the early 1760s. The bell-like sounds produced were made by touching fingers to the wet edges of glass basins.

Clarinet

Glass harmonica

Dance

The minuet

The minuet was introduced in the court of Louis XIV of France, but the dance gained its greatest popularity in the eighteenth century. Noted for its small steps, erect posture, and deep curtsies and bows, the dance was performed by one couple at a time. A couple's turn to dance was based on their social status.

The waltz (left) was first danced in 1794. Using a 3-beat rhythm, the first beat (or step) is strong, while the next two (beats or steps) are lighter: ONE-two-three, ONE-two-three. Created from an Austrian dance known as the ländler, the waltz shocked polite society as the partners held each other close and whirled around the dance floor. It grew, however, to become one of the most well-known of ballroom dances.

Now considered the national dance of Spain, the bolero was introduced in the late eighteenth century. It featured abrupt turns and complicated steps. Often accompanied by a guitar, the dancers sometimes sang and played castanets.

Zoos

Although zoological gardens—quickly shortened to zoo—have been around for thousands of years, the modern zoo is credited to the Imperial Menagerie at the Schönbrunn Palace in Vienna (left), which began in 1752. It opened to the public in 1765. Although a zoo's main objective had been the study of animals, many grew to simply be a source of family entertainment.

Museums

The Louvre museum in Paris

Museums have long held works of art, as well as historic and scientific objects. Many great modern museums had their beginnings in the eighteenth century. The National Museum in Naples, Italy, opened in 1738, featuring paintings and sculptures from Pompeii and Herculaneum.

The British Museum in London opened in 1753, but visitors had to apply in writing for admission. The Louvre in Paris became the first great public art museum, opening in 1793. In America, the Charleston Museum in South Carolina opened in 1773, devoted to the area's natural history.

Games

Charades, a game where words or phrases are acted out in pantomime until guessed by other players, originated in France in the eighteenth century.

Similar to the ancient Chinese game of mah-jongg, dominoes were introduced to Europe in the mid-1700s. Original playing pieces had ivory faces backed by ebony, thus resembling a hooded cloak called a domino.

Sport

The ball and bat game of cricket (left) was believed to be a substitute for dueling in eighteenth century England. The 1744 Laws of Cricket provided very specific game rules. It was the unwritten codes of honesty and good sportsmanship that were firmly incorporated into the game.

Yachts, boats designed for pleasure and sport, were first built for Dutch nobles and merchants in the early seventeenth century. By 1720 the first known formal yachting organization, the Cork Water Club, now the Royal Cork Yacht Club, was founded in Ireland.

Boxing, once an ancient Greek sport, had a comeback in eighteenth century London. Bare-knuckle prizefights were held where men fought for money and spectators bet on the outcome of the fight. The first heavyweight champion was James Figg in 1719. John Broughton, once himself a champion, created the first set of rules in 1743.

Inmates at Fleet Prison in London passed time playing rackets (right) in the eighteenth century. This game of hitting a ball against the prison walls grew into the games of squash and racketball.

The earliest reference to rounders, the ancestor of baseball, was made in *A Little Pretty Pocket-Book* (1744). Players used a hard ball that was hit with a round, wooden stick. The game was played on a field resembling a modern-day baseball diamond. Player positions included a batsman (batter), three post fielders (infielders), two deep fielders (outfielders), and a bowler (pitcher).

THE 1800S

During the nineteenth century, the world seemed to become more settled and more tame. Entertainment, on the other hand, grew wilder. Unbelievable circuses, extraordinary magicians, and breathtaking roller coasters amazed and astounded people. Women began to participate in sports.

Circus

Phineas Taylor Barnum (1810-1891) purchased the American Museum in New York City and went on to create a circus, which he advertised as "The Greatest Show on Earth," starring such acts as the midget General Tom Thumb and Jumbo the elephant. In 1907, after P.T. Barnum's death, the famous Ringling Brothers purchased the circus.

A poster for the greatest show on earth, the Barnum and Bailey circus. P.T. Barnum and James Bailey merged their shows in 1881.

Magic

Magic became respectable entertainment. French magician Jean Robert-Houdin (1805-1871) was a master illusionist and often considered the father of modern magic. Magicians performed for kings and commoners. John Henry Anderson (1814-1874), the Wizard of the North, is believed to be the first magician to pull a rabbit from a top hat.

Jean Robert-Houdin

Games

In 1875, a British Army officer in India created snooker, a game similar to pool. Snooker was the nickname for military cadets in England at the time.

Poker (right), a gambling card game, was popular in the American West and is still wildly played today. The home of the game is believed to be New Orleans. Dead Man's Hand refers to the pair of eights and pair of aces held by Wild Bill Hickock, when he was shot in the back in 1876.

Music

In 1846, Adolphe Sax took a clarinet's mouthpiece and an oboe's keywork and fixed them to a brass tube with a flared bell at the end. This became the saxophone, an instrument whose strong sounds added power to the woodwind section of military bands. It also became hugely popular in pop and jazz music.

The mouth organ, or harmonica, was created in the 1820s, developed from the Chinese mouth organ called the sheng. Its sounds are often heard in folk and country-western music.

Dance

The polka, a folk dance from Bohemia, became a ballroom craze throughout Europe and the Americas.

Puppets

Punch and Judy puppet shows became well-known to people of the 1800s. Sometimes presented as hand puppets and sometimes as string marionettes, the shows were often violent, with Punch wielding a club or stick against the other characters.

Books

Dime novels were first published in 1860 by Irwin P. Beadle & Company. At a fixed price of 10 cents, these paperback fiction books were exciting tales of the Wild West, pioneers, detectives, romances, and rags-to-riches successes. Well over 40,000 titles were printed.

Sport

In America, boat shows traveled up and down rivers, presenting circus acts. One of the most famous boats, the Floating Palace, could seat 2,400 people in its ring.

Rugby was first played at Rugby School in 1823. William Webb Ellis, the first player to pick up and run with the ball during a soccer game, became the inventor of the sport. Originally, rugby balls were rounder, but they gradually elongated into a football shape, making it easier to run with and throw.

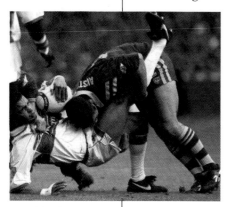

Rugby

Soccer, known as association football in Europe, originated in England in the 1800s. The first professional league, the Football League, formed in 1888.

Canadian football began as a sport similar to rugby, which reached Canada in the mid-1800s. The first organized Canadian football teams played in the Canadian Rugby Union (CRU), founded in 1891.

The first recorded public indoor ice hockey game took place in Montreal's Victoria Skating Rink in 1875. By the late 1800s, ice hockey competed with lacrosse as Canada's most popular sport.

A Japanese educator, Kano Jigoro, developed a wrestling style known as judo in 1882. The idea behind many of the moves is to use an opponent's power against him or her.

Judo

Croquet, played with a mallet, was popular in the late 1800s. Its popularity dimmed with the rage of lawn tennis. Lawn tennis was popular with both men and women in the 1870s. It was called sphairistike, the Greek word for ball game. This was shortened to sticky.

Badminton (right) is a court or lawn game played with lightweight rackets and a shuttlecock. The game is named for Badminton, the estate of the English dukes of Beaufort. It grew popular in America in the 1870s.

Le Volant.

Norway was the homeland of modern sports skiing. The Norwegian Ski Association was formed in 1883, and the first tournament was held in 1892. The sport's popularity was increased greatly by Norwegian explorer Fridtjof Nansen's written account of his 1888 ski trip across Greenland.

From the French velocipedes of the early nineteenth century came the safety bicycle (right). With wheels of nearly the same size, the bicycle's stability was much better. The bicycling craze in America in the late 1800s resulted in the improvement of roads and even affected women's fashions.

The first professional baseball league, the National Association of Professional Base-Ball Players, was formed in 1871. In 1876, the National League (NL) of Professional Baseball Clubs was born. Baseball, however, would not become a popular spectator sport until the next century.

In December 1891, James Naismith (right) developed a new game that would keep his school's athletes busy during the winter season. Nailing a peach basket to the balcony at each end of the gym and making use of a soccer ball, Naismith divided the 18 young men into two teams and created Basket Ball (then two words).

Amusement Parks

In 1817, France created the first roller coaster with cars that lock to the tracks. This was the beginning of safe coastering and led to the development in 1827 of Pennsylvania's Gravity Road roller coaster—the longest and largest coaster ever built in North America. Once a coal mine railroad track, it had an 18-mile (29-km) continuous-circuit route that drew people from miles around.

In 1884, Lamarcus Thompson built the first amusement railroad in the world. His Switchback Railroad (left) at Coney Island consisted of a pair of wooden undulating tracks on a structure 600 feet long (183 m). A train started at its highest point and ran down-grade and up until it lost momentum. Passengers got out while attendants pushed the train over a switch to a somewhat higher point on the second track. The passengers boarded the train again and rode back to the starting point.

THE 1900S

The twentieth century was the age of technology. From the first cars to the space age, people watched with awe and wonder as the world opened up. Musical recordings, motion pictures, cartoons, radio, and television all added to the world's entertainment. Board games grew into video games. Sports turned into big business. Computers became sources of education and fun.

Sport

Football became popular on American colleges in the late 1800s and early 1900s. One of the most physical of sports, 18 college players were killed and over 150 badly injured in 1905. This led to changes in the rules about protective clothing to make the sport safer. Professional football teams became popular after the National Football League (NFL) was formed in 1922. The first Super Bowl, which decides the NFL's champion, wasn't played until 1967.

The Canadian Football League (CFL) was formed in 1960, replacing the CRU as governing body of professional football in Canada. The CFL decides its champion in the Grey Cup game.

Professional ice hockey took a giant leap when the National Hockey League (NHL) was formed in 1917. It included teams from America and Canada. The NHL decides its champion in the Stanley Cup Finals.

In 1901, the American League (AL) was formed to rival the National League in professional baseball. Modern Major League Baseball (MLB) had begun. The first World Series, matching the American League champ against the National League champ, was played in 1903. This rivalry resulted in the rise of baseball's popularity, as it became known as America's national pastime.

Professional basketball became popular after the formation of the National Basketball Association (NBA) in 1949.

Table Tennis, or Ping-Pong, was first played between two British university students using cigar boxes as bats and a champagne cork as a ball. Originally, the paddles were made of plain wood, but in the 1920s, the paddle was given a studded rubber face that enabled a player to put a spin on the ball.

Roller skating became popular in the 1930s with the building of indoor rinks. In the 1980s, in-line skates offered faster, more agile skating. An offshoot of this sport was the skateboard, which went from rough boards of the 1950s to wild plastic or fiberglass boards of the 1990s.

Babe Ruth (below), the "Sultan of Swat," hit 60 home runs in 1927. Ruth was baseball's first superstar.

Magic

Harry Houdini (right) was an escape artist and magician who became one of the famous showmen of all time. His "challenge" act—escaping from handcuffs, straightjackets, and prison cells—brought him fame in the early 1900s. Later feats included escaping from a water torture cell, and walking through a wall.

Amusement Parks

Coney Island in Brooklyn, New York, opened its modern high-speed roller coaster in 1907. Figure-eight coasters were the rage in the early 1900s, but this coaster featured higher lift hills, steeper and deeper drops, and higher speeds.

Disneyland was opened on July 17, 1955. Situated in Anaheim, California, the park spreads over 85 acres (34 ha) of land. Soon Disneyland expanded its original 18 attractions to the present number of 60.

These attractions are divided into seven main themes, including Main Street USA, Adventureland, Frontierland, Liberty Square, Fantasyland, Tomorrowland, and Mickey's Toontown.

October 1, 1971, marked the opening of Walt Disney World in Orlando, Florida. Covering 47 square miles (122 sq km), Walt Disney World is about the size of San Francisco. Of the more than 30,000 acres (12,140 ha), less than one-fourth has been developed. Another quarter of the land is designated as a wilderness preserve.

This castle is the entrance of Fantasyland, one of the sections in Disneyland. This photo was taken on July 5, 1955, as the castle was nearing completion. The castle is called the Sleeping Beauty Castle.

An aerial view of the final stages of construction of Disney World's EPCOT Center with geosphere (center), monorails, and exhibition halls. EPCOT, the city of the future, opened on October 1, 1982.

Superman: the Escape (right), at Six Flags Magic Mountain in Valencia, California, was the tallest and fastest roller coaster in the world at the end of the millennium. At its highest point, it stood 415 feet tall (126 m). It could accelerate from 0 to 100 mph (160 km/h) in seven seconds.

Radio

Radio signals were first used as ship-to-shore communications as early as 1897. Amateur radio sent songs, music, and voices across the airwaves from 1910-1917. While the U.S. was involved World War I (1917-1918), the navy took over all broadcasts to prevent radio's use by spies. But in 1920, KDKA in Pittsburgh broadcast the Harding-Cox Presidential election, and commercial radio began. By the 1930s, news, sports, singing, variety shows, comedies, mysteries, soap operas, science fiction, westerns, and more filled the airwaves.

Families gathered around the "wireless" to listen to their favorite show. This is a "cathedral" radio.

The Jack Benny Program premiered in 1932. Creating an image of himself as a wealthy miser, Jack Benny's comedy show would be one of the top rated programs, continuing until 1955 when he moved to television.

Orson Welles' radio show, The Shadow, *became one of the most popular mystery/detective shows of the century.*

Games

Board games continued to be popular. In 1933, Charles Darrow created Monopoly, the all-time best-selling game. Closely followed was Scrabble, a game of crosswords and spelling, created by American Alfred Butts during the early 1930s.

Pinball machines became popular in the 1930s in drugstores, restaurants, and arcades.

Nolan Bushness, founder of Atari, developed Pong, a black and white electronic table tennis video game in the early 1970s. In 1975, the game was released for home use, which began a national video game craze.

Video game computers such as Atari, Sega, Nintendo, and many others were hooked up to TVs. Top games such as Pac-Man and Super Mario Brothers could be played at home, instead of going to an arcade.

The Sega Dreamcast

Hand-held video games, which use liquid crystal displays, became popular on long trips, as well as short school bus rides.

Virtual reality and 3-D games have been created whereby players can actually interact with the game.

Motion Pictures

For the first 20 years of motion picture history, most silent films were only a few minutes in length. The first film story, *The Great Train Robbery*, was created by Edwin S. Porter in 1903. It was so popular that hundreds of small theaters called nickelodeons, which charged the customer a nickel for a show, sprang up in America. This was the dawn of the movie industry.

French film production led the world in the first decade of the twentieth century. Charles Pathe's newsreels, shown in theater chains, helped him establish the first film empire.

Silent films reached greater complexity and length in the early 1910s. By the 1920s, a new genre had developed, the slapstick comedy, of which Charlie Chaplin was its biggest star. In 1927, the first movie with sound appeared, putting an end to the silent film era.

Stars powered the American Studio System from 1934 to 1946. Various studios, such as 20th Century Fox (1935), Paramount Pictures (1912), Metro-Goldwyn-Mayer (1924), Columbia Pictures (1920), and Warner Brothers (1923) held long-term contracts with both directors and stars. Musical comedies and song-and-dance films were popular.

A major source of revenue for the studios was their ownership of large theater chains. But in 1949, the studios were forced to sell their theaters because of laws against monopolies. The advent of television in the 1950s and the ability of actors to work for a number of studios led to the demise of the old studio system.

In the 1950s, drive-in movies and science-fiction films became popular in America. In Europe and Asia, the trend was toward realism.

During the late 1960s, American studios churned out youth culture movies that attracted younger audiences in record numbers. In the 1970s, the science-fiction and adventure genres, with their emphasis on special effects and sound, became popular.

Thanks to the rise of the cable and home-video industries, independent movie producers flourished in the 1980s. By the end of the millennium, American science-fiction and action-adventure films, with their sophisticated special effects, dominated the industry.

The Birth of a Nation *(1915, right), about the Civil War and its aftermath, was the first of the great American epic films and a landmark in the development of the motion picture.*

The Jazz Singer *starring Al Jolson (left) became the first full-length movie with sound in 1927. His big line: "You ain't heard nothing yet!"*

Walt Disney (right) made his first animated cartoon, Steamboat Willie, *in 1928. His first feature-length animated motion picture,* Snow White and the Seven Dwarfs, *appeared in December 1937.*

Child star Shirley Temple (left) made 25 movies in the 1930s, becoming the decade's biggest box-office attraction.

Acclaimed for its innovative narrative structure, photography, and sound track, Orson Welles' first feature, Citizen Kane *(1941, right), tells the story of a publisher's rise to power. It is considered by many critics as the greatest movie ever made.*

Star Wars (1977, left) became a landmark science fiction fantasy for its use of computerized special effects.

Titanic (1997, right) is a romantic tale of a rich girl and poor boy who meet on the ill-fated voyage of the "unsinkable" ship. The movie's use of computerized imaging helped it become the highest-grossing movie of all-time, earning over $600 million.

Music

Although Thomas Edison created the first phonograph in 1877, recorded sound didn't become popular until the twentieth century. Records gave way to 8-track tapes and cassettes, which gave way to the popularity of CDs (compact discs)—all holding the popular songs of the time.

Ragtime was the first truly American style of music, bridging the gap between European and American music. Ragtime became popular at the beginning of the Progressive Era. Ragtime is believed to be a mixture of European classical music, especially late Romantic music, and African American folk music dating back as far as slavery.

The blues seem to be heavily rooted in African American work songs, field hollers, and spirituals dating back to the first days of slavery. The lyrics dealt with the basic problems and hardships of life, such as poverty, racism, and love, and provided an interesting perspective into the lives of African Americans. With the introduction of the blues came the use of instruments as voices themselves, and not simply for accompaniment.

Jazz began to emerge as a common art form on the streets of New Orleans, as pianists began playing syncopated versions of ragtime songs and waltzes. The first jazz recordings were made by the original Dixieland jazz band led by Nick La Rocca in 1917.

With its roots in the folk music of nineteenth century American settlers, country music had its first success in the 1920s with such artists as the Carter Family and Jimmie Rodgers. In 1925, the *Grand Ole Opry* broadcast its first program from Nashville. In the 1950s, television made stars of country performers like Ernest Tubb, Chet Atkins, and Hank Williams.

The 1930s and 1940s are often referred to as the swing era. Swing music had a smooth, up-tempo, expansive sound. It abandoned smaller groups like trios and quartets in favor of much larger groups of 15 or more members, known as Big Bands.

Elvis Presley

The Bee Gees

Rock-and-roll music evolved from rhythm and blues music. Such people as Bill Haley, Elvis Presley, and the Beatles popularized rock music in the 1950s and 1960s. It remained the most popular music form to the end of the millennium.

Disco music and dancing was a craze in the 1970s and 1980s. Rap music, music that is spoken to a beat, became popular in the 1990s with such rappers as M.C. Hammer.

M.C. Hammer

Dance

Dancing and dance marathons continued to be popular in the twentieth century. The cakewalk of the early 1900s broke the traditional pattern of turns and glides found in European round dances. The ballroom tango became the rage after 1912. The Jazz Age of the 1920s featured flappers who danced the Charleston. The jitterbug dominated the 1930s and 1940s, while the twist helped usher in the rock-and-roll era.

In the mid-1970s, disco dancing brought a return to dancing with a partner in choreographed steps. Acrobatic break dancing (right) was a hit in the mid-1980s.

Web Surfing

Web surfing on the Internet, a vast connection of computer resources from around the world, has become a way to play, do research, write letters (email), order goods and services, and bring the world to one's own computer.

Television

Television became a popular form of entertainment in the late 1940s. Most TV programming was live, and consisted of variety shows, dramas, quiz shows, news broadcasts, and sporting events. By the end of the 1950s, most programs were filmed or recorded on videotape.

The 1960s brought color to television. Although people with black and white televisions could still see the shows, the producers regularly announced: "In Color!" Within 10 years, very few black and white televisions were being made.

People came to know and love television characters and shows. The final episode of *M*A*S*H* (right), a comedic drama on mobile army surgical hospitals during the Korean war, continues to hold viewership records.

Variety shows with songs, jokes, and a number of individual acts grew to great popularity in the 1960s and 1970s. *The Sonny and Cher Show* was one of the most popular (left).

The 1970s and 1980s introduced video cassette recorders (VCRs). Didn't have time to see a movie when it was in the theater? Now it was available anytime you wanted to rent or buy the cassette.

The turn of the millennium has brought the newest in technology, the Digital Video Disc (DVD) player (right). Suddenly, viewers have a crystal-clear movie in wide-screen format with Dolby Digital audio. They have fingertip access to a menu of items such as director's notes, interviews with the stars, language choices, as well as immediate skips to different points in the movie.

High-Definition Television (HDTV, right), provides twice the resolution of a standard TV, as well as a wider screen.

Some early video cassette recorders

40

"Uncle Miltie" brought his crazy gags to American television in 1948 in the variety show, Texaco Star Theater. *A very visual comedian, TV gave Milton Berle the format he needed to not only make people laugh, but to make television a success. He later became known as "Mr. Television."*

I Love Lucy, *starring Lucille Ball and Desi Arnaz, was one of TV's top-rated programs from 1951 to 1957. This sitcom continues to be broadcast nearly 50 years later.*

The soap opera The Guiding Light *made its debut on the radio on January 25, 1937. The show moved to television on June 30, 1952, and was still seen daily through the end of the millennium, making it the longest running soap opera. The cast is shown here in a recent photo.*

Johnny Carson, shown here with Doc Severinsen (left) and Ed McMahon (center), first appeared on The Tonight Show *in 1958 and became the permanent host from 1962 to 1992. The talk show was one of NBC's biggest moneymakers. During the airing of Carson's last show in 1992, an estimated 50 million viewers tuned in.*

MTV debuted on cable television in 1981, broadcasting music videos. Alan Hunter, Nina Blackwood, Mark Goodman, J.J. Jackson, and Martha Quinn (left to right) were among the first VJ's to host MTV.

By the end of the millennium, The Simpsons *had become the longest running prime-time animated series in television history.*

ENTERTAINMENT

1000	1050	1100	1150	1200
People play board games such as tafl; traveling professional musicians; scops travel and tell stories; gleemen travel and sing songs; riddling is popular		Troubadours and minnesingers become popular; viele and organistrum developed; Feast of Fools is popular; bearbaiting is popular sport; Henry I brings Arabian stallion from Spain (1110)	London's Smithfield Track is first modern public racecourse (1174)	

1400	1450	1500	1550	1600
Ballet begins in Italy and France; clavichord is popular; first playing cards; card suits introduced; golf, sport fishing introduced; ice slides invented; archery contests held; Henry V takes minstrels to war (1415)	Johannes Gutenberg prints Gutenberg Bible (1455); Louis XI buys billiard table (1470)	Traveling performers, court jesters; opera invented in Italy; tennis originates in France; rapier introduced in Italy; jai alai begins in Spain; Will Sommers entertains Henry VIII	The modern violin (1550); Shakespeare writes first play (1589); Jacopo writes first opera (1597); Shakespeare becomes co-owner of Globe Theater (1599)	

1800	1810	1820	1830	1840	1850
Soccer; Barnum's "Greatest Show on Earth"	First locking roller coaster cars (1817)	Harmonica invented (1820s); rugby invented (1823); Gravity Road Roller Coaster built (1827)		Saxophone invented (1846)	

1900	1910	1920	1930	1940	1950
Ping pong; baseball; Cakewalk; dance marathons; *The Great Train Robbery*, first World Series (1903); high-speed roller coaster (1907)	Pathe creates newsreels; amateur radio becomes popular; ballroom tango (1912); *Birth of a Nation* (1915); first jazz recording, the National Hockey League (1917)	First commercial radio broadcast (1920); the NFL (1922); Grand Ole Opry (1925); first movie with sound: *The Jazz Singer* (1927); first animated cartoon: *Steamboat Willie* (1928)	Pinball machines; rollerskating; swing music; the Jitterbug; Scrabble; Monopoly (1933); first full-length animated feature: *Snow White and the Seven Dwarfs* (1937)	Television; *Citizen Kane* (1941); *Texaco Star Theater* (1948); the NBA (1949)	

MILESTONES

Fair of St. Denis in Paris, France; carol-dancing performed; music becomes polyphonic; miracle plays are performed; ring-spearing tournaments and blind man's bluff are popular

Chaucer writes the *Canterbury Tales*; pear-shaped lutes are made; Italian harpsichord; falconry and hunting are popular; Noh drama invented in Japan; Tarot cards invented (1320)

Indian rope trick witnessed (1355); Motokiyo perfects Noh drama (1374)

1200	1250	1300	1350	1400

Japanese puppet theater, ten-pin bowling invented; field hockey, lacrosse, acoustic guitar, mask theater, pleasure parks become popular; Kabuki theater begins in Japan (1603)

Vauxhall Gardens open in England (1661)

Clarinet (1700); pianoforte (1709); first yachting club (1720); minuet, bolero introduced; charades, rounders, rackets invented; European composers write masterpieces; pantomime becomes popular

British Museum (1753); glass harmonica (1760s); Imperial Menagerie (1765); circus ring (1768); Charleston Museum (1773); the Louvre (1793); waltz (1794)

1600	1650	1700	1750	1800

First dime novels (1860)

Lawn tennis, badminton become popular; snooker created in India (1875); the National League (1876); Edison creates the first phonograph (1877)

Barnum merges his circus with Bailey (1881); Jigoro invents judo (1882); first amusement railroad (1884)

Naismith invents basketball (1891); first ski tournament (1892)

1850	1860	1870	1880	1890	1900

Drive-in movie theaters; science fiction movies; rock music; Elvis Presley; skateboards; *I Love Lucy* (1951); Disneyland (1955)

The Canadian Football League (1960); The Beatles; color TV; first Super Bowl (1967)

Pong; disco music; Walt Disney World (1971); *Star Wars* (1977)

In-line skates; Break dancing; EPCOT Center (1982)

Rap music; High-Definition Television (HDTV); *Titanic* (1997)

1950	1960	1970	1980	1990	2000

GLOSSARY

acoustic - a guitar whose sound is not electronically modified.

advent - when something comes into use.

amber - a hard, translucent fossil resin that ranges in color form yellow to brown.

archeology - the scientific study of human life.

archery - the art, practice, and skill of shooting a bow and arrow.

bejeweled - ornamented or decorated with jewels.

castanets - a percussion instrument that consists of two connected pieces of wood, plastic, or shell that are clicked together with the fingers.

centrifugal force - the force that flings things outward from the center of a rotation.

chariot - a wheeled, horse-drawn cart of ancient times.

concertmaster - the leader of the first violins of an orchestra who is also usually the assistant to the conductor.

conch shell - the spiral-shaped shell of a large mollusk.

conjurer - a person who practices magic and illusions.

continuous-circuit route - a route without interruption.

contortionist - a person who can twist his or her body into unusual positions.

Crusades - military expeditions undertaken by European Christians in the eleventh, twelfth, and thirteenth centuries. They wanted to win the Holy Land from the Muslims.

curtsy - an act of respect made by women that consists of lowering the body by bending the knees.

deem - to come to think something.

designate - to indicate and set apart for a specific purpose.

discus - a wood or plastic disk that is thicker in the middle than at the edges and is thrown for distance at track and field events.

duel - formal fight between two people fought with weapons in front of witnesses.

8-track - a recording tape that runs on a continuous loop that is divided along its length into eight sections, or "tracks."

elongate - to get or make longer.

epee - a sword with a bowl-shaped guard and a rigid, triangular blade that has no cutting edge and a sharp tip.

exotic - having the charm and fascination of the unfamiliar.

falconry - training hawks to hunt in cooperation with a person.

fencing - the art and practice of attack and defense with an epee, foil, or saber.

ferocious - extremely fierce.

flapper - a young woman in the decade after World War I who showed freedom in conduct.

foil - a sword with a circular guard and a flexible, rectangular blade with a blunt tip.

genre - a category of art, music, or literature characterized by style, form, or content.

gladiator - a person engaged in a fight to the death for the entertainment of ancient Romans.

grisly - inspiring disgust, distaste, or fear.

harpsichord - a piano-like instrument with two keyboards and two or more strings for each note.

headdress - an often elaborate covering for the head.

illusionist - a person who practices illusionary effects.

infantry - soldiers trained and equipped to fight on foot.

inmate - a person confined, as in prison.

innovative - something done in a new way.

javelin - a slender shaft at least 260 cm (102 in) long, thrown for distance at track and field events.

jess - a short strap on a hawk's leg that a leash is attached to.

jester - a person kept in households to provide entertainment.

jongleur - a medieval entertainer proficient in juggling, acrobatics, and music.

joust - to engage in combat on horseback using lances.

kingly - something befitting a king.

liquid crystal display - an organic liquid that forms a crystalline pattern and refracts light like a crystal.

lute - a guitar-like stringed instrument with a pear-shaped body.

lyrics - the words to a song or poem.

mah-jongg - a Chinese game played by four people that uses pieces like dominoes called tiles. The object is to build sets of tiles by drawing, changing, and discarding them.

manipulate - to manage or organize skillfully.

marionette - a wooden figure that is made to move by moving attached strings or wires.

markswoman - a woman who is skilled at shooting.

martial arts - a group of fighting skills developed in Asian countries.

masterpiece - a supreme intellectual or artistic accomplishment.

midget - a person of small size whose body is well proportioned.

mime - to act a part with exaggerated gestures and usually without words.

minnesinger - a German poet and musician in the twelfth, thirteenth, or fourteenth centuries.

minstrel - a person who sings in accompaniment to a harp.

monopoly - the complete control of a product or service.

monorail - a railway system in which the cars run on a single, above-ground track.

Morse code - a system of dots and dashes used to transmit messages over a telegraph.

mosaic - a picture made up of many small pieces, such as glass or stone.

motet - a kind of polyphonic music composed for a choir that is usually sung without accompanying instruments. Polyphonic music has two or more separate melodies played or sung in harmony at the same time.

narrative - a story, experience, or account.

newsreel - a short movie about current events.

oboe - a double-reed woodwind instrument that has a high tone.

originate - to start or bring into existence.

panpipe - a primitive musical instrument. It is a series of short pipes cut off at different lengths and bound together. The player blows into the pipes to make music.

pantomime - a performance where the story is told through only facial expressions and body movements. No words are used.

parliament - a group that makes a country's laws.

penance - a punishment that is usually self-imposed. It is meant to show forgiveness for a sin or other offense.

phenomenon - a fact or event that is observable.

physics - a science that deals with matter, energy, and their interaction.

playwright - a person who writes plays.

precious gem - a rare and valuable stone, such as a diamond.

predecessor - a person who comes before another person, usually in an office or position.

professional - the description of a job that requires special training or education.

proverb - a short saying that expresses a truth.

psaltery - an ancient, stringed musical instrument.

Puritan - a person who belonged to a Protestant group in England in the sixteenth and seventeenth centuries. The group had high morals and wanted simpler religious ceremonies.

rage - a fad, fashion, or craze.

realism - showing people, events, or things as they are in real life.

reed pipe - a pipe organ. It produces its sound when a reed beats in vibrating air.

Renaissance - a revival of art and literature that began in Italy in the fourteenth century.

renowned - famous.

resolution - the level of picture quality on a television set.

revival - the act of bringing something back into use.

rodeo - a public performance of events, such as calf roping, horseback riding, and steer wrestling.

rook - a chess piece that may move any number of spaces parallel to the board's sides.

saber - a sword used in fencing that has a full cutting edge on one side and a partial cutting edge on the back of the tip.

saga - a long detailed story that is usually about a hero or an adventure.

scholar - a person who attends school or studies under a teacher.

secular - not connected with a church or religious order.

self-defense exercises - specific movements that people are trained to use in order to protect themselves if they are attacked.

shamisen - a Japanese musical instrument with three strings.

shogun - a Japanese military governor.

shuffleboard - a game in which players use long cues to push disks down a smooth court.

slapstick - a kind of comedy that uses exaggerated movements.

sophisticated - developed to a highly complex level.

sound track - a recording of the music that accompanies a movie, play, or television show.

squash - a game in which players use rackets to hit a rubber ball within a walled court.

subdeacon - a clergyman below a deacon.

syncopated - a temporary change in a music's rhythm in which the weak beat is stressed.

synonym - a word with a meaning similar to another word.

tarot - a set of playing cards used for fortune telling.

technology - the practical application of knowledge in a particular area.

terra-cotta - a fired clay that may be glazed or unglazed.

troubadour - a lyric poet that was popular in Europe from the eleventh to thirteenth centuries. Troubadours were famous for their love poems.

undulating - moving in a wavelike manner.

up-tempo - music with a fast tempo. Tempo is the speed at which music is played.

vandalism - the act of damaging or destroying property on purpose.

virtual reality - an environment in which a person and a computer are connected. The person's actions can determine what happens in the environment.

Zen Buddhism - a Buddhist group in Japan that believes in enlightenment through meditation.

INTERNET SITES

The Middle Ages
http://www.learner.org/exhibits/middleages/artsentr.html
Listen to medieval instruments. Learn about medieval
storytelling. Contribute your own stories.

Vaudeville and Popular Entertainment, 1870-1920
http://lcweb2.loc.gov/ammem/vshtml/
Links to information about Houdini, sound recordings, theater
playbills and programs, early motion pictures, and English and
Yiddish playscripts. Also discusses types of variety shows.

The Ancient Olympics
http://www.perseus.tufts.edu/Olympics/
Take a tour of ancient Olympia, read about ancient athletes'
stories, learn about the context of the Games and the Olympic
spirit. This site also discusses ancient and modern Olympic
sports.

Piano History
http://www.uk-piano.org/history
This site is sponsored by the Association of Blind Piano Tuners.
Learn about the history of the piano, piano tuning, and piano
pioneers.

*These sites are subject to change. Go to your favorite search engine
and try "entertainment" for more sites.*

FOR FURTHER READING

Anderson, Dave. *The Story of the Olympics.* New York:
William Morrow, 1996.

Ardley, Neil. *Music.* New York: Alfred A. Knopf, 1989.

Granfield, Linda. *Circus: An Album.* New York: DK
Publishing, 1998.

Morley, Jacqueline. *Shakespeare's Theatre.* New York: Peter
Bedrick Books, 1994.

Oleksy, Walter G. *Entertainment.* New York: Facts on File,
Inc., 1996.

Parkinson, David. *The Young Oxford Book of the Movies.* New
York: Young Oxford Books, 1995.

INDEX